CHARLEMONT'S
LA BOXE
FRANÇAISE
&
ENGLISH
BOXING

From Les Sports Modernes Illustrés
1905

Translated by Matthew Lynch 2018

CHARLEMONT VS. CASTÉRÈS
LA SALLE WAGRAM, PARIS.

LA BOXE FRANÇAISE
&
ENGLISH BOXING.

It was the Greeks who first made the art of battling with the fists a regulated exercise which they called *pugilat.* Later they would come to adopt a derivative of *pugilat* which was a mix of wrestling and boxing known as *pancrace*.

English Boxing. - The English have continued the ancient tradition. Around the 14th century they introduced Greek pugilism into their country and it took on the name of *English Boxing.* Since that time it has continued to develop to the point that it now constitutes their national sport.

It is practiced in two different fashions: In the first, known as *sparring,* we see a relatively courteous fight where the fists of both fighters are covered in leather gloves padded with horsehair.

The second is *fighting* with bare knuckles or very light gloves that are hardly padded. These fights make for sensational matches and enormous wagers. Even at matches featuring the most famous opponents it is rare to see one of the fighters succumb. These bloody fights are, moreover, banned in almost all countries and have become more and more rare.

English boxing has not found much of a foothold in France where the reception for a sport that is all about power and brutality is lukewarm, and the practice of which requires a very particular type of endurance.

It is moreover a circumscribed form of combat that calls into play the fists alone. Head and body holds are forbidden, as are wrestling moves. This is the case in fights or matches regulated by the rules of the Marquis of Queensberry (*Queensberry Rules*), although there are other sets of rules wherein holds are allowed, but these are rarely seen.

La Boxe Française. – French boxing has not existed for a full century. It made its appearance in 1824 under the name of *Savate*. Of its origin we know little. We know only that it refers to a kicking art and that it was above all honored by the brawlers of Old Paris. The professor Charles Lecour added punches to *Savate*. Charlemont senior and son perfected the art and made it what it is today. It encompasses punches, kicks, head holds and body holds. It makes use, in a word, of all of the means a man has to defend himself. One can define it as the *art of personal defense*. It is all about flexibility, skill, and agility. It is a recreational exercise and it is relatively easy. It is easy from the point of view of the effort required, for it does not require athletic movements, as each limb moves with its own momentum and does nothing it was not meant to do by nature.

If sparring- for in French Boxing there really is no *fighting* per se- offers a means for the martial artist to perfect his skill more or less indefinitely, we can also say that lessons in the sport are easy to follow even for a heavy and unathletic individual, allowing him to make better use of his limbs even when he has attained a ripe old age. Moreover in a simple lesson where we limit ourselves to the various conventional movements and phases of *La Boxe Française,* the average person will find sufficient interest to the extent that the practice become fun.

La Boxe Française from a physical education perspective.- As a form of physical education the best kind of sport is the least specialized. This is to say we would not want a sport that works with a limited region of the body, or which brings into play, to the exclusion of all others, a particular aptitude such as strength, or agility, or speed. Now from this point of view French Boxing is the least specialized of all exercises because it calls into action all of the muscles of the body while developing the other physical aptitudes, not focusing on one particular facet to the detriment of the others.

In French Boxing the leg must be used as energetically as the arm, the left side must be used as often as the right and, as a consequence, all members and regions of the body are worked equally. The practice of this sport does more than harmonize the muscular forces. The boxer acquires other qualities which are of an order that fits between the physical and intellectual planes. We can even say without exaggeration that the practice of sparring gives constant exercise to a number of intellectual faculties: level-headedness, hand-eye coordination, and mental toughness.

In adults and children alike it combats timidity. It modifies our reaction in moments when courage is needed-- in a word, the *sang-froid* we acquire lends us energy and bravery.

A word on fitness.- We have come to see that French Boxing is the type of exercise which develops the body evenly. We can further say that it is the sort of activity which can correct the body when it has the tendency to deviate. It is a true gift in terms of orthopedic health.

If the sport gives certain benefits to children and young people, it gives others to the grown man and the man older man. At the age of forty or fifty the most frequent health troubles faced by a man who works in an office or a businessman are those arising from a lack of exercise. Most of these troubles have something to do with the digestion. Now among the factors giving rise to such disorders, we notice first and foremost an atrophy of the abdominal muscles. Nature has foreseen and, so to say. discounted the action of these muscles, since it is their action which must ensure the mechanical milling of foodstuffs.

For this reason we find that men given over to hard physical labor, those who bend and rise one hundred times per hour, and all of those who earn their daily bread through hard toil will tend to have a good digestion, while the idle man, or at least the physically idle man, finds himself inert for hours after a meal.

If we wish to conserve the vigor and firmness of the abdominal muscles, if we wish to strengthen them and so oppose the deposition of fatty elements which lend the sedentary man his *"flat tire"* --which is after all but food that cannot be digested-- then we must work these muscles daily with appropriate exercise.

Now French Boxing is a sport which works the abdominal muscles. Whether he is delivering a kick or a punch, evading a blow or throwing one, the abdominal wall of the boxer is always working.

La Boxe Française is a sport as much adapted to ameliorating the most common conditions of age as it is to fighting the most common vices facing young people in the process of growth.

Is La Boxe Française dangerous?- It is not dangerous to practice *La Boxe Française*. Since its inception there has not been one serious incident. There will be the occasional black eye and even that is rare. Bruising is common during sparring, but as for lessons there is nothing to fear. French Boxing is taught like grammar, drawing, and music.

***La Boxe Française* as self defense.-** French Boxing has retained its original character as a form of defense, which is after all its *raison d'etre.* While giving students a means to have success in combat, it also lends them grace, elegance, and good posture. The power of the strikes taught in French Boxing is enough to dispatch one or several inexperienced adversaries.

Sparring sessions.- The exterior manifestations of *La Boxe Française* are displayed in public sparring sessions. Sparring is not fighting, it is simulated fighting.

Public sparring sessions which are subject to various rules to be listed later on are generally organized by the various clubs that have formed to promote the sport. These displays tend to win new students to French Boxing. In sparring sessions the fighters are not so much looking to land a good shot as they are to display their skill, flexibility, and dexterity. The blows struck with precision give the public an agreeable impression of the beauty of the exercise while offering them a sense of what such athletes could really do in the case of a fight with such tools at their disposal.

PRACTICING
LA BOXE FRANÇAISE

We do not pretend to write a full treatise on boxing. Here you will simply find a well-reasoned collection of the most important moves.

The Guard: The guard is the position we assumed when facing the opponent, a position which offers the most advantages both offensively and defensively. In this position you should be relaxed and free from muscular tension.

There are 2 kinds of guard:

1. *The left guard* in which the left side of the body is set forward.

2. *The right guard* in which the right side of the body is set forward.

Right handed people prefer the right guard and left handed people prefer the left guard.

All exercises are performed in both guards by turns such that both sides are used equally, allowing left and right to acquire the same skill and power. If one side is less strong and adroit than the other, which is almost always the case, it is imperative to work that side until equilibrium is established.

Left Guard (fig. 1, below): The left foot is set forward with the toes facing ahead. The right foot is set back and to the left with the toes facing the right, with about 40 centimeters between the two feet. The position should be such that if you pass the right heel forward it would graze the interior of the left foot.

The legs are slightly bent, the bodyweight resting on the right leg with the upper body somewhat inclined to the rear.

The left shoulder is forward, the left arm stretched forth in front of you and slightly bent, the hand closed and placed at the level of the shoulder,

Fig. 1: The left guard & the right guard.

The fingers turned up with the thumb above the fingers.

The right shoulder is drawn back somewhat with the right forearm placed almost horizontally near the chest without touching it. The fist is closed at the level of the left elbow and near it without touching it and the fingers are turned up. The head is straight with the eyes fixed on those of your opponent. In this position the left arm covers the upper body and the right arm the lower body.

The Right Guard: This is the same as the left guard in reverse (*see fig. 1*).

True & False Guard: Two opponents are in true guard when they face one another in the same guard. They are in false guard when they are in different guards. It is often very advantageous to throw certain strikes from false guard.

Advancing & changing guard: Advancing and changing guard while advancing allow you to approach the opponent can cause him to retreat and diminish the space behind him leaving him less free to move. In this way you can hamper his movements and so paralyze his defense.

Stepping back and falling back by switching guards allow you to create distance and avoid rapid attacks without resorting to arm blocks. You can also use these as feints.

Switching guard to advance: Pivot on the left heel so as to bring the right half of the body forward. In this way you find yourself in the right guard.

Move forward: Bring the right foot close to the left foot and immediately bring the left foot forward to the usual distance with the arms and body not changing position.

Move back: To retreat bring the left foot beside the right and immediately bring the right foot back to the usual distance with your body and arms remaining in position.

It is essential to advance or retreat as we have indicated, since if you advance by bringing the left foot forward you expose yourself to a low kick the moment your foot touches down. In your retreat, you face the same situation when you begin with your right foot.

Preparatory exercises for flexibility and balance: It is recommended that a beginner spend several lessons doing a series of solo exercises. These are aimed at making the student flexible and imparting balance, as these are indispensable to the sport.

We cannot offer the complete nomenclature here, as it would occupy too much space. The exercises consist of the combination of all fundamental strikes broken down into their component elements.

KICKS

In our method for *La Boxe Française* there are many kicks. These can be divided into two categories:

Fig. 2: Evading the low kick.

Fig. 3: Evading the low kick & countering with a punch.

The first category includes kicks that are relatively simple to execute, although they do require a certain amount of work to render them fast and effective. They are above all useful from an offensive or defensive point of view. These are:

The low kick.

The chassé-croisé to the body or leg.

The side kick.

The front kick.

The chassé to the body or leg.

The second category of kicks are more difficult to execute, brilliant to watch in sparring, and can in fact be performed by any student with a lot of hard work. They allow those who develop superb flexibility in their legs to perform feats that they never would have dreamed of when they began practicing the first series of kicks. These advanced kicks are:

The kick to the chest.

The kick to the face.

The low or high roundhouse kick.

The back kick.

The Low Kick: The low kick is one of the kicks best suited to combat both for its ease of execution, its quickness, its power, and the surprise it always excites in an adversary who is ignorant of French

Boxing. When thrown with vigor from the false guard it can break the leg when it lands dead center on the tibia. This is how it is done:

The right leg is slightly flexed as you hurl it powerfully straight ahead such that the heel grazes the inner edge of the left foot in passing. Your right instep impacts the center of the adversary's tibia. Your foot is tensed with the toes facing the ground obliquely out to the right. At the same time, throw your arms back on either side of your body and tilt your torso back while arching your back and opening your chest. These movements of the arms augment the impulsion given to the leg while holding the body in perfect equilibrium (*see fig. 2*).

After striking you must return the right foot to its starting point while returning your arms to guard.

Blocking the Low Kick: There are five ways to evade the low kick.

1. *Remove the [targeted] leg.*

2. *Change guard to the rear.*

3. *Use a stopping kick.*

4. *Grab the leg.*

5. *Move the [targeted] leg.*

The first evasion is performed with your body weight resting on your right leg. Lift your left leg and bring your left ankle as close to your left buttock as possible with the foot pointed, the toes facing down, the arms and body immobile (*see fig. 2*).

Using this evasion puts us in a position, once the opponent has struck at nothing, to respond immediately with various strikes such as the *low kick,* the *side kick,* the *kick to the chest,* the *kick to the face,* the *chassé* to the body or leg, the *chassé-croisé* to the body or the leg, the *back kick,* and the *roundhouse kick.*

The second evasion involves switching guard to

the rear to buy time if you are taken by surprise.

The third evasion involves throwing your own *chassé-croisé (see the explanation for stopping-kicks below)*.

The fourth defense would be to *seize the leg (see below)*.

Simply removing your targeted leg is difficult to execute as it demands timing and speed. You have to have foreseen the attack, but when this is the case you will be able to throw a jumping punch to the opponent's face or body (*fig. 3*).

Side kick: The side kick must impact the opponent on his side in true guard and on the abdomen in false guard.

This is how it is done:

1st movement: Turn and face left without moving your head by pivoting on your left heel with your toes directed toward the left. At the same time that your body is turning your arms go along with it while retaining their position such that they find themselves placed to the rear to act as a counterweight to the leg which immediately is raised in front of you. Your body is straight, your back arched, your left leg stiff. To facilitate this rotation of the body you must raise the right heel slightly (*fig. 4*).

2nd movement: Lift the right leg and bend it horizontally in front of you with the foot flexed at the level of the knee, the heel brought up against the thigh (*fig. 5*).

3rd movement: Thrust the leg out horizontally to strike with the toes above the opponent's belt (*fig. 6*).

4th movement: Having struck, belt the leg back while pivoting to the right on the left heel as you bring the right foot back to its starting position with your arms returning to the left guard position.

Blocking the side kick: To block the side kick thrown with the right leg you must quickly lower your left forearm without moving your left elbow and strike the top of the incoming foot with your fist so as to drive it to the left. When training you should block the foot with the inside of the open hand so that you do not hurt the student's leg with too many hard strikes (*fig. 6*).

The side kick, like the *chassé-croisé* or the *chassé,* can be parried by the *outside parry.* We can also seize the leg with one or both hands (*see leg grabs, below*).

Counters to follow blocking the side kick: Having parried the side kick you can counter by one of the following strikes:

You can throw a left punch to the face with a jump, a punch to the body or face with your right while lunging or stepping in, a horizontal punch to the body with your right, a low kick, a side kick, a kick to the chest, a kick to the face, a *chassé* with your

right foot to his body or leg, a jumping *chassé-croisé,*

a back kick, or a roundhouse kick.

Fig. 4 (bottom) & 5(top)- Side kick, movements 1 & 2

Outside parry: This parry has the advantage of causing the opponent to lose his balance while making him spin so that he presents his back, allowing you to counter with different strikes such as the body punch, the face punch, the low kick, the *chassé* to the body or leg, the *chassé-croisé*, and the back kick.

The outside parry is performed by bringing the right foot back 10 about centimeters and withdrawing your hips such that your body is beyond the range of the strike. At the same time pass your right hand over and behind the striking leg at the level of the ankle, then chase the leg off to the right with a vigorous push. You can profit from the opponent's loss of balance by throwing the counters named above.

Kick to the chest: This is the same as the kick to the side, save that is delivered to the chest. It is only thrown from false guard as this is when the opponent's chest is vulnerable (*fig. 7*).

Block a kick to the chest: From right guard facing an opponent in left guard, you must parry by striking the top of his right foot with your open right hand, your fingers together, your forearm almost vertical, the elbow down (*fig. 7*).

You can also seize the incoming leg with both hands.

Countering after blocking a kick to your chest: After you parry the kick to your chest you can counter with a left punch to the face while jumping, a jumping *chassé-croisé,* or a *chassé* to his body with your right leg.

Kick to the face: This is executed is the same manner as the kick to the side save that the blow must be delivered to the opponent's face.

Parry the kick to the face: This block is the same as that for that for the punch to the face (*see fig. 8*).

Counters after blocking a kick to the face: After having parried a kick to the face you can counter with a right to the opponent's face or body, a low kick, a *chassé* with your left leg while jumping, a *chassé-croisé* while jumping, or you can seize his leg with both hands.

Front kick: The front kick is not allowed in sparring since it is very dangerous, but it is a very practical kick for the street where it is delivered to the genitals or the stomach when an attacker comes in with a head-butt to your chest. It is delivered by raising your right thigh, bending the lower leg in and bringing the knee to belt level with your toes facing the ground. Your upper body should be somewhat inclined toward the rear. Extend the right leg forward in a straight line to strike with the tip of the shoe, impacting the attacker's lower abdomen. Bring both of your extended arms back behind you on either side of your body. Now bring the right foot back to its point of departure and return to guard.

Parry the front kick: This block is the same as the one used for the kick to the body, but here we strike from high to low on the incoming leg. You can also grab the leg by passing the left hand under it to lift it as high as possible in order to bring about a fall. You can also seize the leg with both hands, for leg grabs see page 79.

Countering the front kick: You can reply to this kick with all of the strikes indicated for the kick to the body.

Chassé-croisé: This is one of the most formidable kicks which when delivered to the body with the heel can move a larger opponent and even him knock him to the ground. It can also be delivered to the leg, and when applied to the knee it can smash the joint.

The chassé-croisé while advancing: This kick is only practiced in solo exercises. You must first turn to the right and bring your arms behind you to the right. At the same time your left foot, pivoting on the heel, is placed crosswise and parallel to the right with the toes facing right. Place your bodyweight on your right leg while you bend the left. Cross the legs by passing the right leg behind the left such that the right foot is placed a bit in front of the left and parallel to it. Lift the left leg and bend it in front of you with the knee as close in to your body as possible, the foot bend such that the heel is foremost at knee level. Extend the left leg forward on a horizontal line to strike with the heel (*see fig. 10*).

Jumping chassé-croisé: Cross the legs by passing the right leg behind the left while the right leg itself pushes the body into the air and the left thigh comes to be placed as close as possible to the abdomen. Extend the left leg vigorously to strike the adversary's body as the

Fig. 6 & 7: Kick to chest (top) & side (bottom).

right foot returns to the ground. Return to

guard by allowing the left leg to replace the

right, which moves to the back at the proper distance for the guard position.

Block the chassé-croisé to the body: The block for this kick is the same as that used for the kick to the side. You can also use an outside block, or put your hands together and strike the incoming foot from high to low. You can also grab the leg with both hands or use stopping strikes.

Chassé-croisé to the leg while jumping: This is executed in the same manner as the *chassé-croisé* to the body save that it is delivered to the tibia, knee, or thigh.

Block the chassé-croisé to the leg: Block this kick with your arms or evade with your leg and counter with a punch to the face or body. You can also use the horizontal punch, the *chassé* stopping kick, and leg grabs.

Counters: You can counter with all of the strikes mentioned for the kick to the side.

Fig. 9: Loading up the chassé-croisé

Fig. 10: The chassé-croisé delivered with the heel.

Fig. 11: The back kick.

The Chassé kick: The *chassé-croisé* contains the *chassé*. It is delivered by a direct extension of the leg and strikes with the heel. It can be thrown from standing or while jumping with the lead leg or the rear leg. It can be aimed at the body or the legs.

To throw the ***rear leg version***, turn your body to the left as with the first motion of the side kick and at the same time position the leg as you would for the third motion of the *chassé-croisé while advancing (fig. 9)*. Now execute the fourth movement for the *chassé-croisé while advancing*. Here we also bring the left foot forward to gain space all while commencing with feigned punches.

For the ***rear leg chassé while jumping***, you must leap forward with your left leg while you raise the right leg to strike. This allows you to follow a retreating opponent and, should he be a bit off balance, he will fall to the ground.

For the ***lead leg chassé*** you must first execute the third movement of the chassé-croisé while advancing (*fig. 9*). Now execute the fourth movement of the chassé-croisé while advancing (*fig. 10*).

The **lead-leg jumping chassé** is performed like the standing chassé save that at the moment the left leg is raised you must jump with your right leg to gain ground.

Block and counter the chassé kicks as you would the side kick (*fig. 6*).

Back kick: This is one of the sweetest kicks in La Boxe Française. It has great effect in sparring but it is difficult to master as it requires great flexibility in the legs, excellent timing, and precision to succeed.

It can be executed with the lead leg or the rear leg, from standing, leaping, or even while turning (a very difficult feat).

The ***rear leg back kick from standing*** is performed by turning on the left foot as you would for the side kick while throwing the right leg to the left such that it describes an arc between your left foot and the opponent's face. Now strike his face with the sole of your right foot (*fig. 11*).

For the ***lead leg back kick*** you must throw the left leg to the right while turning on your right heel such that you describe an arc running from your right foot to your opponent's face. Now strike his face with the sole of your left foot.

Both of these kicks can also be performed with a leap from the supporting leg in order to gain ground.

A ***jumping back kick*** is executed with the lead leg and the same commencement as that used in the jumping chassé-croisé, but in this case the foot, instead of going directly to the body, impact's the face after having described an arc in the manner explained above.

The blocks for the back kick are like those used for a straight kick to the face.

Roundhouse kick: This is also a great kick to use in sparring, but it too is difficult to execute. Executing this kick as a solo exercise is an

Training with Charlemont

excellent lesson in balance. If it is not very practical as a self-defense kick, it can at times be used to throw a heel to the body or the leg. It is useful above all when employed as a stopping kick.

First, turn to the right on both heels while making a half turn such that your right shoulder comes forward and your left shoulder moves back. Your head is to the right facing the opponent.

Now execute the third and fourth movements of the chassé-croisé while advancing (*fig. 9, 10*).

You can *use it as a stopping kick* in the case where you throw have thrown a kick to the opponent's side and he employs the outside block, then seeks to reply with a punch. We profit from his parry by setting out right foot on the ground while lifting the left leg and turning to the left to strike the opponent in the chest the moment he steps in. Of course, this must be done quickly to succeed.

To *block and counter this kick*, you should use the same methods as you would for the side kick if it is aimed at your body. If it is aimed at your leg, evade as you would with a low kick. A chassé stopping kick is also useful when delivered above the belt in this case at the moment the opponent presents his back, and you should be able to topple him.

LEG GRABS

It is not as easy as you would think to grab a leg thrown by a good fighter, and less so to keep hold of it once you have it. Yet is you can do this, the leg grab allows you to topple the opponent or unbalance him while you throw counters with fists and feet.

To *grab a low kick from the right leg* you must squat quickly to snatch it at the ankle with your left hand. At the same time bring your right foot about 30 centimeters to the right and back, your left leg straight and your weight resting on your bent right leg.

From here you can pull the opponent to you to make him fall forward. Now release the leg and throw a right punch to his face (*fig. 12*).

Fig. 12: Grab the low kick

If your leg is trapped, you can disengage by turning to the left while leaning back and pulling the leg violently toward you. Correct your stance and return to left guard.

When a right kick comes in to your body, grab the ankle with your left hand and pull it toward you to make the opponent fall forward. Now release the leg and throw a left punch to his face.

To escape you can use the method employed for the low kick.

The two-handed grab is used for all kicks. Grab the leg with your two crossed hands like a pincer, the left hand down holding the end of the foot, the right hand over the leg holding the ankle near the heel. Lift the leg up as high as you can and switch guard to the rear while tilting your torso back. If the opponent is not completely unbalanced by this, throw a low kick to knock out his supporting leg.

There are five ways to escape from the two-handed leg grab.

1. As soon as your leg is grabbed, draw your leg in powerfully and throw one or two punches to the opponent's face.

2. Draw the leg in and then thrust it out vigorously.

3. If you are about to fall, place your hands on the ground and pull the leg to you to draw the opponent in, then fire a kick to his face with the heel of your free leg.

4. Having set your hands on the ground while dragging in the trapped leg, use your free leg to strike his lead leg with your foot turned crosswise.

5. Having set your hands on the ground, draw in the trapped leg and thrust it out vigorously into the opponent's chest.

These last three escapes are used as a last resort when you absolutely cannot remain standing.

To grab a front kick, snatch the foot with your left hand under the heel and the right hand over the foot. At the same time, switch your guard to the rear in order to unbalance the opponent. Now briskly shift your guard forward, pushing the leg forward in order to overturn your opponent (*fig. 15*).

Fig. 12: Grabbing the low kick.

Fig. 13: Two-handed leg grab.

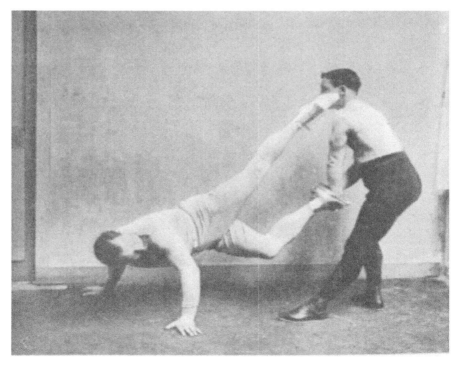

Fig. 14: Escape with a kick to the face.

Fig. 15: Snatching the front kick.

STOPPING STRIKES

Stopping strikes are those which impede the development of an opponent's strikes and so render them ineffective.

Students who are adept at these strikes can embarrass the best fighter is a sparring match.

In a real fight these can be used to advantage since they require very little space and, as you do not have to move in order to strike, you remain sure of your balance which allows you to receive energy without stumbling.

Stopping strikes are delivered with the lead leg when the opponent is close and the rear leg when he is far. Punches are also used in this way.

You can use a lead leg chassé as a stopping kick for a low kick or a low chassé-croisé. As soon as the low kick or low chassé-croisé is initiated, strike the attacking leg using the mechanics of the chassé-croisé while advancing (*fig. 17*).

When faced with a chassé to the body, a jumping lead leg chassé, or a low kick, you should execute your stopping kick using the mechanics of the jumping lead leg chassé.

This stopping strike cannot be executed save by jumping since when the low kick is delivered from a distance since it is impossible to reach him by staying in place.

Fig. 16: A 'coup de pointe' stop strike.

Fig. 17: Stopping the low kick.

The *lead leg chassé to the body* can be used to great effect in a fight when executed against an opponent who throws out his upraised arms to seize your neck, arms, or body.

In sparring it is used against all manner of punches and kicks.

It is executed using the mechanics of the third and fourth motions of the chassé-croisé while advancing (*fig. 9. 10*).

The *rear leg chassé stopping kick* to the leg is executed by attacking an opponent's leg as he initiates his low kick. If he throws some other kick, throw your rear leg chassé to his body using the mechanics of the advancing chassé-croisé (*fig. 9, 10*).

The *coup de pointe* is delivered with the tip of your shoe to his stomach when he throws a punch to your face or a low kick. Just as with a kick to the body, you should use your lead leg to strike.

The *front kick* is used as a stopping kick to strike the opponent's abdomen when he tries to grab your legs or head-butt you in the chest.

A punch to the face is a stopping strike often used against another punch (*see section on punches below*).

A punch to the body with your lead hand while jumping is sometimes used as a stopping strike against a side kick or even a chassé-croisé delivered slowly.

Fig. 18: the 'coup de pointe' stopping the low kick.

Forking: This is a method used against high kicks that come in slowly. It is not often used due to its difficulty, but when done well it places the opponent at your mercy. It is done in the following way:

At the moment when the striking leg reaches full extension, pass your left forearm under it and hook it with the inside of your elbow. Lunge forward on your left leg at the same time and immediately bring your right leg inside of and behind the opponent's left leg. Put your forearm up under his chin to shove him over backwards, and at the same time lift his right leg with your left arm (*fig. 20*).

PUNCHES

It is essential to be well versed in the art of punching. Punches are the indispensable

Fig. 19: Punch & Parry.

Fig. 20: forking

complement to kicks. Moreover, throwing punches is an excellent way to develop the upper body.

From a defensive point of view punches are the most useful tool and play the main role in combat when space is too limited for the legs to enjoy freedom of motion.

In English boxing as it is practiced in Britain and the United States the left guard is prefered. We think it better to train the left and right guard, and the Marquis of Queensberry, with whom we trained in English and French boxing for almost twenty years, was of the same opinion. At that time he tried to popularize the idea in England and America, but he was up against entrenched habits and his words fell on deaf ears.

However some strikes are more effective in false guard than in true guard, and you can confuse many an English boxer accustomed to maintaining the left guard by switching guard at will.

Some punches are only effective at close range, and they cannot be used in French Boxing where the legs hold an opponent at a distance. There are times, however, when you can land such punches when the time is right.

In French Boxing we often use the arms for feints so that a kick can be thrown immediately, and the opposite also occurs.

For a punch to have power it must first land with a firmly contracted fist, striking with the metacarpals and not the phalanges. The wrist must be straight or it will be sprained. The shoulder and the rear leg add to the impetus of the arm (a punch comes as much from the leg as from the arm) and the body accompanies the striking arm. The arm must also remain supple and not contract until the moment of impact. In this way we channel the efforts of the entire body at a single moment.

Fig.21: Body-blow & block.

The hardest and most decisive blows in a fight are those delivered to the jaw near the chin, to the neck at the carotid, and to the chest near the heart or sternum. All of these strikes produce bewilderment such that a man will "crumble like a house of cards" and sometimes lose consciousness.

These are the strikes that professional English boxers seek to land in order to "finish" their opponents.

The guard position is the same in English Boxing as it is in French Boxing, though they tend to hold their upper bodies somewhat inclined forward.

Feints are often used in attacks in order to bring the opponent's attention to a place where the attack will *not* be delivered, and in this way he will expose a target that *can* be attacked.

Thus a boxer will feign a punch with one arm and strike with the other, feign a punch to the face to strike at the body be it with that same arm or the other. There are also feints used to induce the other boxer to strike, and in this case a stopping strike or counter punches can be thrown. One can also use feints to make an opponent strike and miss, at which point the boxer evades and throws a punch to the head or body. A boxer must become used to countering quickly after blocking or slipping.

Punches can be delivered from standing, lunging, advancing or jumping.

They are divided into:

The straight punch to the face, the straight punch to the side or body, and the horizontal punch to the face or body. These are avoided by blocks and slips.

In the beginning it is good for students to break the punch down into parts and exaggerate the movements in order to develop punching power and because the student is always tempted, in sparring, to minimize movement in order to move more quickly.

Straight punch to the face from standing: First bend the left arm by drawing the elbow back along with the shoulder while opposite shoulder comes forward. Bend the legs somewhat while keeping the torso upright.

Now throw the left arm directly forward at the adversary's face while taking a small step forward with your right leg such that your upper body is brought forward. In this way the weight of your body accompanies the strike and empowers the impact. At the same time bring the bent right arm to the rear along with the shoulder. This motion adds to the power of the strike given with the left hand (*fig. 19*).

Now resume your left guard.

It goes without saying that in actual practice all of these motions occur almost at once and as quickly as possible.

Blocking the straight punch: When a left straight punch comes in, pass your right forearm (hand closed, fingers forward) under and inside of the opponent's left forearm, forcing it to the right and somewhat forward. At the same time bend your left arm to make ready for your counter.

When countering it is good practice to lean back with your upper body to increase the security of your block (*fig. 19*).

This block is the simplest which is why it is the one that is most often used. However there are others which demand more skill and precision. The *outside block* is performed with the left arm, fist closed, against a left. The *inside block* is performed with the open left hand against an incoming left. These three blocks or parries have the advantage of unbalancing the opponent and facilitating your counters.

Counters to a punch to the face: After blocking you can respond by a punch to the face, a body-blow, or a horizontal punch to the body or face with a bent or extended arm.

Straight punch to the body: This punch is executed with the same mechanics as the punch to the face but it is delivered to the body.

Blocking the straight punch to the body: The parry is executed in the following way: When a left comes in, pass your right forearm over and inside of the opponent's left forearm, striking with your wrist to drive the arm to the right (*fig. 21*). You can also parry by striking the opponent's left forearm from the outside with your right wrist, driving it to the left.

The horizontal punch: First you must stretch the right arm out behind you without stiffness. The hand is clenched and the fingers are turned in toward the body (*fig. 22*). Now throw the arm forward along a horizontal arc so as to strike the opponent on the face or body (*fig. 23*). When using this punch it is best to set it up with a feigned left which will hide the windup.

When two opponents are sufficiently close

Fig. 22: Initiating the horizontal punch

Fig. 23: Horizontal punch & block.

the arm can also be drawn completely to the rear and the punch delivered while recruiting the shoulder, be it with a bent or a straight arm.

Blocking a horizontal punch to the face: This block is the same as the one used against the straight punch (*fig.23*)

Blocking a horizontal punch to the body: This block is the same as the one used against the straight punch to the body (*fig. 21*).

Lunging punch: The lunging punch uses the mechanics of the standing punch, but here we lunge 30 centimeters forward with our left foot.

Punch while advancing: This is a rear-hand punch executed while shifting your guard forward. At the moment when your bodyweight shifts from your right leg to your left, the punch extends forward as you bring your whole upper body forward.

Punch while jumping: This punch is used often in *La Boxe Française* since it allows one to attack from the outside. As a direct attack it is delivered with your lead hand, but you can deliver it with your rear hand if you first throw a feint with your lead hand.

To execute the punch your legs must be slightly flexed. Jump from your rear leg as you throw your upper body forward. Your left leg is placed in front and the right is set behind it at the usual distance.

The punch must land at the moment when the left foot touches down.

Blocks: The three punches named above are blocked like a standard punch to the face or body.

Slips: Slips are movements of the head or body which allow you to avoid punches as the opponent strikes nothing. You can almost always profit from a slip to fire stopping strikes to the opponent's face or body.

If the attack comes from the left arm, slip to the right, and in this way the opponent's arm will be above your left shoulder. Before he can reset you should throw a straight left or a hook to his head or body. If on the other hand you slip *left* when a left comes in you will be open to rights.

You can sometimes slip left with success if you then stop the opponent with a shot to the jaw with your rear hand.

Slip your head right: At the moment a left comes in, bend your head quickly to the right and forward while keeping the opponent in your sight. This motion is enough to let the arm move past your head without touching it.

Slip your head left: The same idea as above.

Slip right with your body: Bend your upper body to the right and forward. At the same time, hit him with left hook or straight punch.

Slip left with your body: The same idea as above, reversed (*see fig. 27*).

Turn side-on: This slip is simply performed by turning your body to the left while throwing a stopping punch to the opponent's face with your right hand.

Fade back: Throw the upper body back by flexing the legs and raising the left heel to facilitate the flexion of the body.

As you return to a full stand you can throw a left to his body (*fig. 28*).

Rotational Slips: This slip flusters the opponent more than all others as he seeks in vain to attack the head that rolls around his arms.

It is performed like a right body slip with a rotational motion from right to left. You pass under the opponent's arm to emerge standing on the other side. Now throw a left.

All of the slips mentioned so far are executed from a static position.

Slip right with a lunge: This is done like the standing body slip, save that you lunge obliquely with your left leg to the right and forward. Now throw a punch to the face or the body with your lead hand (*fig. 29*).

This slip is also performed with the addition of another motion of the leg, which is to say after having lunged with the left leg without throwing a counter, pivot on your left foot and bring your right foot forward as you turn to face the opponent. In this way you find yourself behind him, and from here you can throw a series of punches.

HOLDS & GRAPPLING.

In a street fight where there are no rules, you can naturally make use of all means at your disposal. Thus on top of the various moves we

Fig. 24: Slip head to the right.

Fig. 25: Slip right with the body, left stopping punch.

have indicated above we add some holds or grappling moves which can be very useful in hand-to-hand fighting. Among these the *head and hip throw,* the *belt throw,* and the *force collar* are very useful.

The head and hip throw: Grab the opponent's left wrist while passing your right arm behind his head to hook his neck in the crook of your arm. Pass your right leg in front of his left while turning your back to him. Load him on your right hip to unbalance him and throw him to the ground by pulling violently on his right arm (*fig. 30*).

The belt throw: This is executed with the same mechanics as the prior throw, but in grabbing the opponent by the belt instead of the head.

The Force Collar: When the adversary lowers his head, seize it with your left arm and encircle the neck. Apply your right hand to his neck and squeeze your arms as tight as possible. Doing

*Fig. 26: **Slip right with the body, throw a left.***

Fig. 27: Slip left with the body, throw a right.

Fig. 28: Fade back.

Fig. 29: Slip right with a deep step.

this can suffocate the enemy.

SPARRING IN
LA BOXE FRANÇAISE

Sparring is a means of putting what you
have learned into practice. In your first sparring

sessions you will find yourself disoriented since, left to your own devices with no one to tell you which strike to throw, you must begin to string together attacks and counters. It takes time to be able to read your adversary's game and guess at what he will do.

Hand-eye coordination is key, as the proper execution of strikes depends upon it. It is a natural quality: A teacher can cultivate it, but he cannot impart it. A fighter with few physical gifts who has this one quality naturally has an advantage over a physically gifted opponent who lacks it.

Sang-froid is acquired through practice, speed and skill are gained through exercise.

However limited the physical capacity of a beginner, he will always gain good results so long as he shows perseverance. He may never become a brilliant fighter, but if he works his low kick, his stopping strikes and his punches he will become a formidable adversary.

A gifted student with flexibility and skill can obtain any level he attains to and will be able to execute all of the strikes that we have listed.

FIGHTING

If all of the strikes we have indicated can be executed in sparring, it is not the same as a match in which we most recommend the use of

Fig. 30: The head & arm throw.

the low kick, the chassé-croisé low or high, the side kick, the front kick, the chassé stopping kick to the body and the various punches.

The chassé stopping kick to the body is very practical, as it does not alter balance and can be used in the following case: After having fading back from a punch to the face thrown by an opponent who is too close, we wait firmly with our weight on the rear leg. Without a doubt he will enter in to grab you out of inexperience, trying to wrap you up. Execute the chassé stopping kick with your lead leg, and when done well it will knock your attacker over.

Rules for Sparring in
La Boxe Française adopted by the
Union of French Boxing Clubs.

Art. 1: Matches are overseen by an authorized president assisted or not by vice-presidents, and the fighters must submit to his decisions without question.

Art. 2: Matches take place in one or several rounds the length of which is set by the president. The end of the match is signalled by the president with the words: *Sirs, the final* *point.* At this the fighters resume guard and continue until one of them is struck.

Art. 3: Matches must be courteous and devoid of brutality. At the start and the end of the match the fighters bow to the president and shake hands.

Art. 4: All punches will be delivered above the belt and all kicks from the feet to the top of the head, both in attack and as counters.

Art. 5: Strikes to the arms and forearms when these are not touching the body do not count, but when they are touching the body the strike is valid.

Art. 6: Front kicks and kicks to the lower stomach are not valid.

Art. 7: All strikes must be blocked or evaded before a counter is thrown.

Art. 8: Stopping strikes are allowed and must be clearly defined.

Art. 9: Grabbing the legs does not count unless the hold lasts for several seconds and the fighter cannot free himself.

Art. 10: Tie-ups are illegal.

Art. 11: When a fighter is struck or his leg is grabbed he must announce *touché* in a loud voice– no other word is valid. After this the fighters return to guard and continue.

Art. 12: Fighters who engage in a match governed by these rules as set forth by the *Union of French Boxing Clubs* must acknowledge the rules.

Any fighter can be excluded from a match at a word from the president.

ENGLISH BOXING MATCHES

English boxing as it is practiced in Britain and America has its own special set of rules. It demands greater stamina than skill and knowledge. A match does not stop when a point is scored, and the boxer who can better absorb punches is almost always the winner.

Matches or exhibitions are subject to the rules set down below.

In the matches, fights, or championships between professionals the rules are modified. The weight of gloves varies from 2 to 6 ounces (an ounce is about 30 grams). The fight takes place in a given number of rounds, most often until one of the fighters cannot rise from the ground within 10 seconds.

This last sort of fight is only allowed in certain less populous American states, which does not keep them from being organized within certain private circles.

Rules for Amateur Championships in England according to the "Amateur Boxing Association"

Art. 1: In all open contests the ring must be surrounded by ropes. The ring will not be less than 12 feet square and not more than 24.

Art. 2: The contestants must box in slippers or soft soled shoes (no nails) with short pants and a sleeved jersey.

Art. 3: The weight classes are:

Bantam– no more than 8 stone 4 (53 kg)

Feather– no more than 9 stone (57 kg)

Light– no more than 10 stone (63.5 kg)

Middle– no more than 11 stone 4 (71.665 kg)

Heavy- any weight.

The fighters will be weighed on the day of the match in their boxing attire and without gloves.

Art. 4: In all open contests the result shall be decided by 2 judges and a referee. A timekeeper will be appointed.

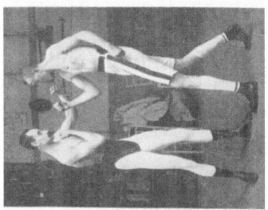

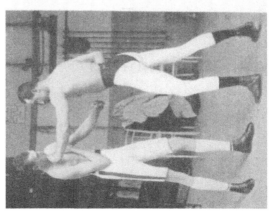

English boxing: Some punches used by Jeffries.

Art. 5: In all open matches there will be 3

rounds. The first 2 rounds shall be 3 minutes

long and the final round 4 minutes. The interval
between rounds will be 1 minute.

Art. 6: In every match, a contestant who is not
present when *time* is called will lose the bout.

Art. 7: In the case where one of the contestants
is unable to fight, the able fighter will face an
adversary chosen by the judges.

Art. 8: All fighters must have one second who
will not advise them during the fight, nor will
anyone else be allowed to advise the fighter.

Art. 9: Judging takes place in the following way:
The two judges and the referee will not confer.
At the end of each fight, each judge will make
known the name of the contestant who has won
in his estimation and give it to a third party. In
the case where the judges are in agreement, the
victor is declared. In the case where the judges

do not agree, the third party will inform the referee, who then decides the outcome.

Art. 10: The referee has the final say when judges do not agree. He has the right to stop a match when a fighter gets knocked down. A stoppage during the first or second round does not keep the third round from proceeding. A referee can also demand another 2 minute round be held when the judges cannot agree on a winner.

Art. 11: The decisions of the judges and the referee are final and cannot be appealed.

Art. 12: In every match the decision must be in favor of the fighter who showed better style and who obtained the greater number of points. The points will be given for *attack:* a clean shot with the metacarpals of either hand to any part of the forehead or sides of the head or the body above the belt. For *defense:* blocks, slips, fades, or stopping strikes. If the total of points is equal, we look to the number of points awarded for *attack* to find the winner.

Art. 13: The referee can, after seeing foul play, disqualify a contender who uses dirty tactics by whipping or striking with the inside of the open glove or the fingertips, or using the wrist or the elbow while tying up or shoving the opponent against the ropes.

Training: To make a good showing at an English Boxing match you must undertake a severe training regimen which varies according to the age of the boxer and the condition in which he finds himself at the time of the fight.

In order to keep himself in psychological shape he must not change his habits too quickly, but modify them progressively. The boxer must seek to attain his maximum of muscular vigor. He must rise early and sleep early and undertake a clean nutritional regime with plenty of grilled meats, green vegetables, and very little liquid [sic], a half glass of wine cut with water, or some beer or tea. He must not smoke or touch liquor. If he is to fat he must do some brisk walking on a daily basis for 2 to 3 kilometers covered in warm vestments to work up abundant sweat. He must workout with light weights to develop the shoulders and arms and jump rope to work the legs. Having thus prepared his body he will work out with the heavy bag, the speed bag, and training partners in order to hit hard and endure the hardest shots without being put out of the fight.

For a professional the training is more rigorous still and can last several months. He generally works with a manager who cares for him like a horse trainer. The manager sees to his affairs, directs his training and oversees all that has to do with his man, with whom he stays until the day of the fight. It is true that in England and above all in the U.S. there is a fortune to be made for the winner of a professional match, and even the loser walks away with a tidy sum.

Among the winners of these famous matches, the best known are:

John. L. Sullivan, Jim Corbett, Bob Fitzsimmons, and J. Jeffries, current champion of the world.

Costume: The best costume for boxing is a pair of flannel or wool leggings or a singlet. These materials are best because they absorb sweat without becoming cold. The leggings should have ample room in the thigh and gather at the calves and the ankles.

A belt of elastic material of about 4 centimeters width should complete the costume and hold the pants in place with fasteners. All large or stiff belts hinder movement and most not be used, as they can lead to hernias, above all among youths. The shoes must be of supple (buffalo) leather that can be laced, with light flat soles. These shoes are the only practical type, as they support the ankle while the foot stays flat and does not slip. The gloves used in *La Boxe Française* must be made of smooth lambskin with cuffs. They are padded with horsehair of the first quality. Thanks to their padding, most blows need not be feared.

We foresee the use of thumbless gloves, as we have remarked that with the thumb sewn in there is a tendency to jamb the digit during a punch. One can also wear shin-guards, but we are not great fans of this, as students who know their shins are safe become to indifferent to the low kick.

BOXING CLUBS

The taste for boxing has become so general over the last 15 years that many gyms have been founded and these have many students.

There are a number of clubs whose sole purpose has been the promotion of the sport.

They have succeeded in drawing more and more adepts by holding annual public and private matches. These clubs include:

La Boxe Française, The Boxing Club of France, The Society for the Promotion of Boxing,

La Boxe Française of Raincy, La Boxe Française of Marseille, La Boxe Française of Roubaix, La Boxe, Parisian Boxers, French Boxers.

These clubs have come together, the first six in the Union of French Boxing clubs, and the three others, to which are added some smaller clubs, have formed the French Federation of Boxing Clubs.

BOXING TERMS

Changing guard: *Movement of the legs allowing one to approach the opponent (forward guard change) or create distance (rear guard change). Guard is changed in order to come to the optimal position for delivering a strike.*

Chassé-croisé: *A kick delivered by jumping and crossing the legs, throwing a leg heel first into the leg or body of the opponent.*

Re-counter: *Counter delivered after blocking the opponent's counter.*

Chassé: *A direct strike to the leg delivered with the heel.*

Stopping strike: *Delivered at the moment a strike is initiated, it stops the opponent's strike.*

Evasion: *Lifting the leg to avoid a low kick or a low chassé, or pulling it in to escape a leg grab.*

Forking: *Toppling the opponent when he kicks by seizing his leg and body.*

Slip: *Movement of the head, body, or leg which allows one to avoid a punch or a high kick.*

To be uncovered: *You are uncovered when your arms are not in guard position to protect your face and torso.*

False attack: *Feigning an attack to induce the opponent to uncover some part of his body.*

Feint: *False attack with the arms or legs.*

Finish: *Deliver a shot that puts the opponent out of the fight.*

Guard: *Position used when facing the adversary which offers the best offensive and defensive advantages.*

Advance: *Approach the opponent with changing guard.*

Block: *Stopping strikes with the arms.*

Leg Grab: *Allows you to topple the opponent.*

Combination: *A series of blows.*

Rounds: *Timed sections of a match.*

Counter: *Strike delivered after blocking a strike.*

Cover: *Place the arms so as to protect the face.*

-END-